SONGS SIGNS AND STORIES
by John Horton

Designed & Illustrated by Michael Kennedy

Pupil's Book Three
ED 11411A

Schott & Co. Ltd, London
48 Great Marlborough Street
London W1V 2BN

B. Schott's Söhne, Mainz

Schott Music Corporation, New York

© 1985 Schott & Co. Ltd, London

ED 11411A

ISBN 0 901938 63 7

DONKEYS

Calling someone an ass or a donkey is like saying he is stupid, or at least obstinate. People also make fun of this patient and useful animal for other reasons, such as his loud, braying voice and his fondness for eating thistles. All the same, the donkey has been much loved and even respected. In eastern lands he used to be given special honour as the mount chosen to carry kings and other great personages. Muslim law forbids overloading the donkey, and there are several stories in the Bible that show him as a trustworthy and intelligent animal. In the Old Testament there is the story of Balak the king, Balaam the prophet, and the ass that spoke. In the New Testament we can read accounts of how Jesus rode on the back of a donkey into Jerusalem, an event remembered in Christian churches on Palm Sunday. A fine old hymn often sung in the Palm Sunday processions goes like this (only two verses are given here, but originally it had *thirty-seven,* so that it could last through a very long procession!):

ALL GLORY, LAUD, AND HONOUR

CHORUS *All glo - ry, laud, and ho-nour To thee, Re-deem- er, King, To*

whom the lips of chil - dren Made sweet ho - san - nas ring.

*Christ mounted
on a donkey*

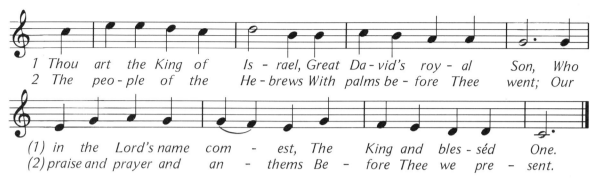

1 Thou art the King of Is - rael, Great Da - vid's roy - al Son, Who
2 The peo - ple of the He - brews With palms be - fore Thee went; Our

(1) in the Lord's name com - est, The King and bles - séd One.
(2) praise and prayer and an - thems Be - fore Thee we pre - sent.

(repeat CHORUS *after each verse)*

Another church procession, with a donkey as its centre, used to take place in France about six hundred years ago. It was held in memory of the journey of Mary and Joseph, with the child Jesus, into Egypt to escape the massacre ordered by King Herod. A donkey richly arrayed, and carrying a young woman with a baby in her arms, was solemnly led along the street, through the great west door of the church, and right up to the high altar, in the midst of a cheering and singing crowd. The choir sang this song, and all the people joined in at the end of each verse:

HERE'S A DONKEY FROM THE EAST

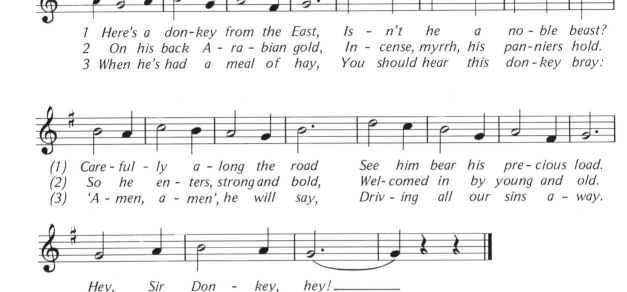

1 Here's a don-key from the East, Is - n't he a no - ble beast?
2 On his back A - ra - bian gold, In - cense, myrrh, his pan-niers hold.
3 When he's had a meal of hay, You should hear this don - key bray:

(1) Care - ful - ly a - long the road See him bear his pre - cious load.
(2) So he en - ters, strong and bold, Wel - comed in by young and old.
(3) 'A - men, a - men', he will say, Driv - ing all our sins a - way.

Hey, Sir Don - key, hey!

A very beautiful but rather sad song in a minor key comes from the mountains of Spain. It mourns the death of a donkey everyone knew and loved:

THE DONKEY'S BURIAL

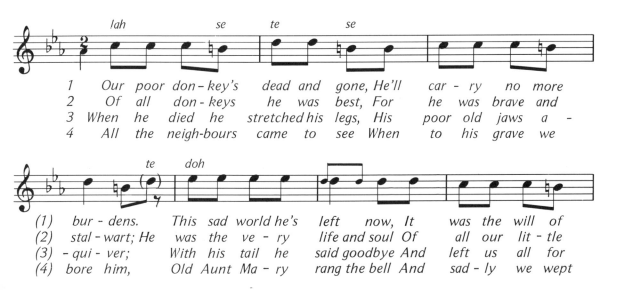

lah   *se*   *te*   *se*

1   Our   poor   don-key's   dead   and   gone, He'll   car-ry   no   more
2   Of   all   don-keys   he   was   best, For   he   was   brave   and
3 When   he   died   he   stretched his   legs, His   poor   old   jaws   a -
4   All   the   neigh-bours   came   to   see   When   to   his   grave   we

te   *doh*

(1)   bur - dens.   This   sad   world he's   left   now,   It   was   the   will   of
(2)   stal - wart; He   was   the   ve - ry   life and soul   Of   all   our   lit - tle
(3)   - qui - ver;   With   his   tail   he   said goodbye   And   left   us   all   for
(4)   bore   him,   Old   Aunt   Ma - ry   rang the bell   And   sad - ly   we   wept

fah *soh*

(1) Hea-ven.
(2) ham-let.
(3) e-ver.
(4) for him.

Sing tu - ru - ru - ru - ru, Sing tu - ru - ru - ru - ru, Sing

me *ray* *me*

tu - ru - ru - ru - ru, Sing tu - ru - ru - ru - ru.

Our last donkey song is an amusing one from Lancashire. It was sung on the decks of the cargo ships that sailed between Liverpool and Canada. The shanty-man, chosen for his good voice and memory and his skill in making up words for a tune on the spur of the moment, started the song and the rest of the men joined in the chorus. The words of 'Donkey-riding' describe all kinds of sights that could never be seen, just as no sailor who had ever made the trip round Cape Horn would believe it could be 'always fine and warm'. As for the idea of bringing donkey-riding into every verse, this may have been put into the shanty-man's head by seeing the men using a steam 'donkey engine' to help with the timber-unloading:

DONKEY-RIDING

1 Were you e - ver in Que-bec Stow-ing tim - ber on the deck?
2 Were you e - ver off the Horn Where it's al - ways fine and warm,
3 Were you ever in Car-diff Bay, Where the folks all shout 'Hooray'!

(1) Where there's a king with a gold-en crown Rid-ing on a don-key?
(2) And seen the lion and the u - ni- corn Rid-ing on a don-key?
(3) Here comes___ John with___ three months' pay Rid-ing on a don-key'?

Hey! Ho! a - way we go Don-key rid-ing, don-key rid-ing.

Hey!___ Ho! a - way we go, Rid-ing on a don - key.

Things to do

1 You can find the story of Balak and Balaam and the ass that spoke in the Old Testament, in the Book of Numbers, chapter 22. You might write the story in your own words, and illustrate it as a strip-cartoon.

2 A hymn book will give you more verses of the hymn 'All glory, laud, and honour' (though not all thirty-seven of them). An interesting thing about the old German tune we usually sing to it is that it is really an English dance tune, *Sellenger's Round.* The tune was probably taken round Europe by English comedians like Will Kemp, and then turned into a hymn tune by slowing it down, putting it into four-beat time, and fitting religious words to it. Before that happened (in the days of the great church reformer, Martin Luther), older melodies were used for the hymn. We know about the Palm Sunday processions in some of the great English cathedrals. For example, in Salisbury the singing used to be started by seven choristers placed high above the south doorway of the cathedral. In Hereford, too, the procession would begin at the cathedral, go through the main streets, and finish up at one of the town gates, on top of which seven choristers were singing the hymn.

3 See if you can find a poem called *The Donkey,* by G. K. Chesterton. It tells the story of Palm Sunday, and the donkey's proud share in it.

V FOR VICTORY

The Morse Code signal for letter V is ••• —

This pattern (three short taps followed by a longer sound) was beaten out on a drum and broadcast all over the world by BBC Radio during the later years of the war of 1939-1945. It was a signal of hope (V for Victory) and was meant to encourage all who were working for freedom, whether openly or in secret.

One way of writing the V signal in musical notes is:

(three one-beat notes and a three-beat note).

Another way of writing the same pattern is:

The dotted crotchet ♩. in this pattern is a way of showing that a one-beat note is going to be split into three equal quavers ♫♪ . If we are still thinking of the Morse Code, ♩. by itself could stand for — or letter T, and ♫♪ for ••• or the letter S.

There is a distress call (S-O-S) which can be signalled in Morse with three dots, followed by three dashes, followed by three more dots ••• — — — ••• This was chosen because it is easy to recognise, and very unlikely to be part of an ordinary word. The same pattern would look like this in musical notes:

Notice that we have given the pattern a special time-signature. We are by now used to $\frac{2}{4}$, and know that it means the beats are to be grouped in twos. When the time-signature is $\frac{2}{4}$. it means that again the beats are to be in twos, but that every beat can be split into three equal quavers.

Now try repeating these two rhymes, one in $\frac{2}{4}$ time and the other in $\frac{2}{4}$. . When you have *said* them, *play* them on a drum (or clap them):

Pan-cake Day, Pan-cake Day, if we can't have a ho-li-day we'll all run a - way.

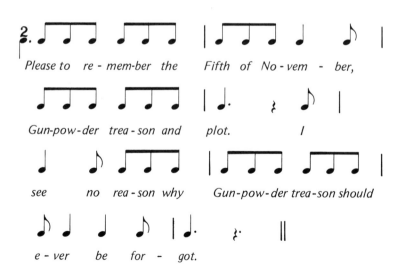

Please to re - mem-ber the Fifth of No - vem - ber,

Gun-pow-der trea-son and plot. /

see no rea-son why Gun-pow-der trea-son should

e - ver be for - got.

There are a few more things to notice about these $\substack{2 \\ \flat \cdot}$
patterns.

A whole beat's silence is shown by a dotted crotchet
rest: ♪·

The pattern *long-short,* which is like the letter N in Morse,
is ♩ ♪ in musical notes. It is really two-thirds of a beat
followed by one third.

Every now and then (but not very often) we have the opposite
pattern *short-long,* which is like the Morse letter A • —
In musical notes this is quaver-crotchet ♪ ♩ , or one-third of
a beat followed by two thirds.

Sometimes we have a two-third of a beat's silence,
followed by a quaver which makes up the rest of the
beat: ♪ ♪

You can find all these signs in the rhyme
'Please to remember'.

Now for a song in $\substack{2 \\ \flat \cdot}$ time. It comes from
Italy, and is about a poor man who longs for
macaroni or other sorts of pasta. It has a
lively dance tune, of the kind called a *tarantella.* People used to believe that the tarantula
spider, which lives in parts of Italy, had a
poisonous bite, but could be driven away
and the bite cured by listening to a tarantella
tune and dancing to it. Sometimes the tune
was played with a tambourine accompaniment.

We have printed the song in the key of
G minor, with a key-signature of two flats,
meaning that *doh* is B flat, *lah* is G; *se*
keeps occurring in the tune, and is shown by
an F sharp:

MACARONI

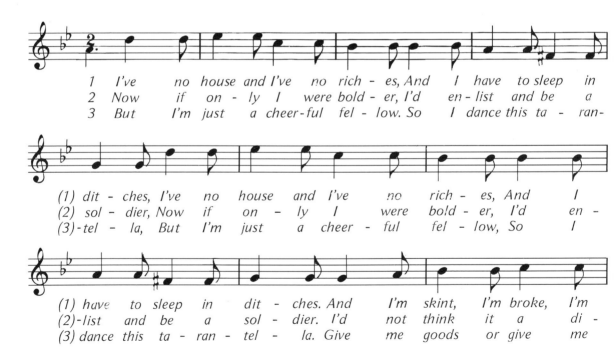

1 I've no house and I've no rich - es, And I have to sleep in
2 Now if on - ly I were bold - er, I'd en - list and be a
3 But I'm just a cheer-ful fel - low. So I dance this ta - ran-

(1) dit - ches, I've no house and I've no rich - es, And I
(2) sol - dier, Now if on - ly I were bold - er, I'd en-
(3)-tel - la, But I'm just a cheer - ful fel - low, So I

(1) have to sleep in dit - ches. And I'm skint, I'm broke, I'm
(2)-list and be a sol - dier. I'd not think it a di -
(3) dance this ta - ran - tel - la. Give me goods or give me

(1) sto - ny, Or   I'd   buy   some ma -   ca - ro - ni. And   I'm
(2)-sas - ter Meet - ing   bul - lets made   of   pas - ta. I'd   not
(3) mo - ney, And I'll   buy   some ma -   ca - ro - ni. Give   me

(1) skint, I'm broke, I'm   sto - ny, Or   I'd   buy some ma - ca - ro - ni.
(2) think   it   a   di - sas - ter Meet - ing   bul - lets made of   pas - ta.
(3) goods or give   me   mo - ney, And I'll   buy some ma - ca - ro - ni.

ROLL THE BALL ALONG

A strong $\stackrel{2}{}$ rhythm is good not only for dancing, but also for any other kind of movement that must go with a regular swing: rowing, for example, or paddling a canoe. 'Roll the ball along' was a favourite with the French traders who explored the rivers of Canada in their canoes. The story of the ducks on the pond and the prince who shot them started its life in France, was brought to the New World by the early traders or *voyageurs,* and spun out for verse after verse to make it last for many hours of paddling. The words, which of course were originally in French and began *'En roulant ma boule',* had nothing to do with fur-trading or canoeing, but they helped to pass the time and keep the paddles going:

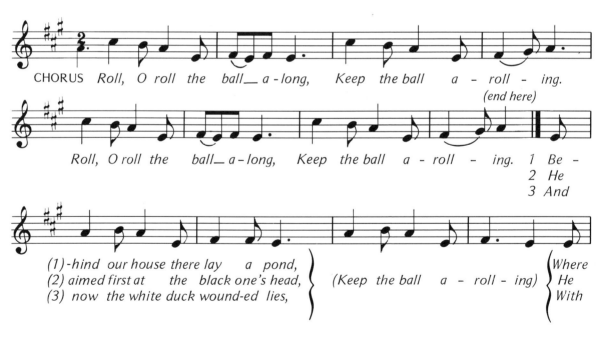

CHORUS *Roll, O roll the ball_ a-long, Keep the ball a - roll - ing.*

(end here)

Roll, O roll the ball_ a-long, Keep the ball a - roll - ing.   1 Be -
                                                                    2 He
                                                                    3 And

(1)-hind our house there lay   a pond,   (Keep the ball   a - roll - ing)   {Where
(2) aimed first at   the black one's head,   {He
(3) now the white duck wound-ed lies,   {With

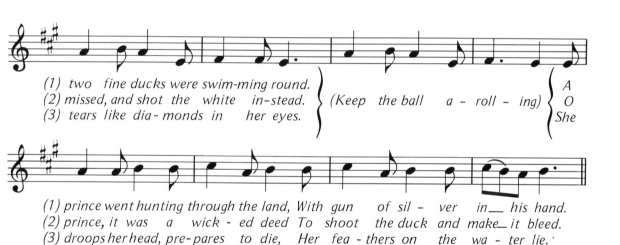

(1) two fine ducks were swim-ming round.
(2) missed, and shot the white in-stead.
(3) tears like dia-monds in her eyes.

(Keep the ball a - roll - ing)

A
O
She

(1) prince went hunting through the land, With gun of sil - ver in__ his hand.
(2) prince, it was a wick - ed deed To shoot the duck and make__ it bleed.
(3) droops her head, pre-pares to die, Her fea - thers on the wa - ter lie.

(repeat CHORUS after each verse)

LOUDER AND SOFTER

We know already that sounds are made by back-and-forward movements in the air called vibrations, and that quick vibrations give higher sounds than slow ones. If the vibration is only a slight back-and-forward movement the sound will be quiet, as you can prove by gently plucking a violin string or lightly tapping a drum. If you pull the string or hit the drum harder it will give a louder sound, *though not a higher or lower one.* In the same way, you can hum a note almost in a whisper, or try to make exactly the same note fill the room.

Music would be dull if all the sounds in it were alike in volume — all quiet or all loud. Quiet or soft sounds are suitable for some music, such as a song about sleep, but we should expect really loud sounds in a musical picture of, say, a battle.

There are special words, borrowed from the Italian language, which remind musicians how much volume to use in singing or playing a particular piece of music (or part of a piece). These are a few of the 'volume' words:

piano (often shortened to *p*) meaning *quiet*
pianissimo (or *pp*)   *very quiet*
forte (or *f*)   *loud*
fortissimo (or *ff*)   *very loud*
mezzo-forte (or *mf*)   *fairly loud*

A *pianoforte* is an instrument that can make quiet or loud sounds, according to the speed at which we move the keys and make the hammers strike the strings.

The volume of sound can change suddenly — perhaps from *piano* to *forte* and back again in a single bar of music. Or the change can be gradual, so that the sound grows from soft to loud, or dies down from loud to soft. The Italian word for 'growing' is *crescendo*, often shortened to *cresc.*, but the sign is sometimes used instead of the word. The opposite word, meaning 'get quieter', is *decrescendo* or *diminuendo (dim.)* and this too has a sign:

Even when there are no Italian words or other signs, we are expected to plan changes in volume or *dynamics* when we make music; it helps if we think what kind of piece it is we are singing or playing, what the words are about (if it is a song), or how the phrases follow one another.

Some instruments, like the recorder, are naturally quiet and it is hard to make much difference of volume with them, though it is a good idea sometimes to have one or two recorders on their own and then make a group answer them — or the other way round. We can do the same thing with a solo voice and a chorus, or a small body of singers and a larger one; this often works well when one phrase echoes another.

Now try speaking this rhyme, which we have called *'Crescendo'*, and gradually build up the volume from a single 'nail' to a whole 'battle'. There can be a sudden *diminuendo* in the very last line. We have used the signs instead of the long Italian words, and to make it easier to fit them in we have stood them on end:

'CRESCENDO'

2. For want of a nail, the shoe was lost,   *pp*

For want of a shoe, the horse was lost,   *p*

For want of a horse, the ri - der was lost,   *mf*

For want of a ri - der, the bat - tle was lost,   *f*

For want of a bat - tle, the king-dom was lost,   *ff*

And all for the want of a horse - shoe nail.   *pp*

19

Things to do

1 Find out how volume of sound is measured scientifically in *decibels.*

2 A sound may become so quiet that only a few people, with very acute hearing, can catch it at all. On the other hand, some sounds are so loud that they become painful and can injure one's hearing. Do you know of any trades or occupations in which the workers have to wear ear-protectors?

3 Here are some pairs of words describing sounds of different volume. Find more words to put in both columns:

whisper	shout
tinkle	boom
chirp	croak
squeak	roar

BLACKSMITHS

Every village of any size used to have a blacksmith's shop or forge, and larger towns would need several 'smithies' where working in iron was carried on. Farm implements like ploughs and harrows had to be made and repaired, tools for every trade put in order, railings for houses and churchyards constructed, and all kinds of iron fittings provided — fire-grates, bolts and latches for doors — and other jobs by the dozen. And, of course, there was the shoeing of horses. A blacksmith who gave most of his time to shoeing was called a farrier; before the days of vets he was expected to know something about animal medicine and surgery. Nowadays there are fewer farriers, and though blacksmiths are still needed for shoeing riding-horses most of them live by making beautifully-designed objects out of iron, like garden furniture and firescreens.

The old blacksmiths' forges were full of exciting and even musical sounds. You could hear all day long the puffing of the bellows, the roar of the fire, the stamping of horses, and above all the ring of hammers on anvils. The strangely-shaped anvil, a block of iron or steel resting on a solid wooden base, made different patterns of sound according to the stage the job had reached, and many of these sound-patterns or rhythms can be heard in rhymes and songs about blacksmiths' work. Try repeating these two rhymes, and playing the anvil-pattern on a metal bar, a steel triangle, or anything else that gives a clear, ringing sound:

John Smith, fellow fine

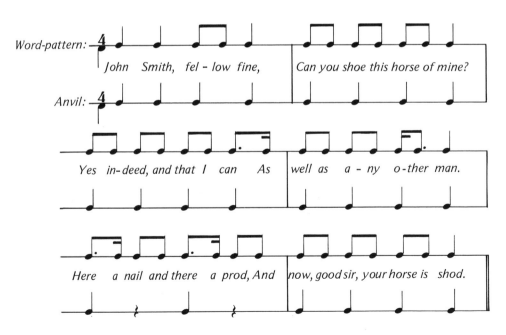

Word-pattern: John Smith, fel - low fine, Can you shoe this horse of mine?

Anvil:

Yes in-deed, and that I can As well as a - ny o-ther man.

Here a nail and there a prod, And now, good sir, your horse is shod.

Who will be the smith's man?

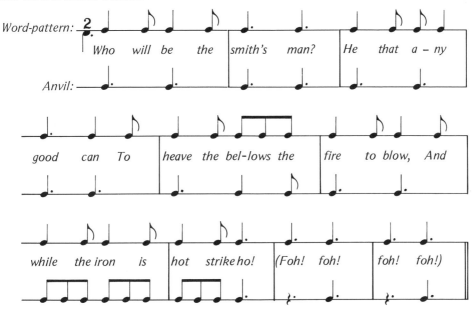

Word-pattern:

Who will be the | smith's man? | He that a – ny

good can To | heave the bel-lows the | fire to blow, And

while the iron is | hot strike ho! | (Foh! foh! | foh! foh!)

Anvil:

(*Foh!* stands for a puffing sound to imitate the bellows)

The blacksmith and his mate often hammered on the same piece of iron with alternate strokes of their hammers. Two people can try these 'duets', using two metal beaters on metal bars or triangles:

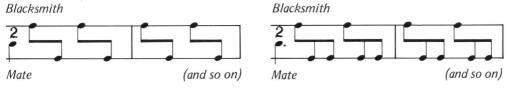

Blacksmith

Mate   (and so on)

Blacksmith

Mate   (and so on)

Now for some songs. The first, from Russia, is a kind of echo song, and sounds best if two groups share it, or better still if one voice leads and the others answer with a phrase that is nearly the same but not quite:

IN THE SMITHY

1 The smi - thy rings with the noise, The smi - thy
2 They strike the iron as it glows, They strike the
3 They work hard all through the day, They work hard
4 'To - mor - row we'll have a rest, To - mor - row

(1) rings with the noise Of the black-smith and his two ap-pren-tice
(2) iron as it glows, And they send the red sparks fly - ing with the
(3) all through the day, Till the week-end comes and then they all three
(4) we'll have a rest, And we'll dress our-selves in all our Sun-day

(1) boys, Of the black-smith and his two ap - pren - tice boys.
(2) blows, And they send the red sparks fly - ing with the blows.
(3) say, Till the week - end comes and then they all three say:
(4) best, And we'll dress our - selves in all our Sun - day best.'

The other song is a fine old English one, though some of the words take a bit of puzzling out. Somehow or other the 'bellows' have been changed into 'bagpipes', and the 'green willow' is hard to explain; one suggestion is that binding the nozzle of the bellows with fresh willow twigs was a way of keeping it air-tight:

TWANKYDILLO

1 Here's a health to the black-smith the best of all
2 Here's a health to King Char - lie and like - wise his

(1) fel-lows, Who works at his an - vil while the boy blows the bel-lows;
(2) queen, And all the royal chil-dren where - 'er they are seen;

(1,2) Which makes my bright ham-mer to rise and to fall. Here's to

old Cole and to young Cole, and to old Cole of all: Twan-ky-

-dil - lo, twan-ky-dil - lo, twan-ky - dil-lo, dil - lo, dil - lo, dil - lo. A

roar-ing pair of bel - lows made of the green wil-low.

Things to do

1 Enquire if there is a blacksmith's forge near where you live or are on holiday. You might ask to look in at the door and watch the work going on, and see how the fire, the bellows, the anvil, and the many different tools are used. If you know a riding school, you might find what arrangements are made for the horses and ponies to be shod.

2 Think of the solution to this riddle in rhyme. How are the 'four elements' of Fire, Water, Earth, and Air used in blacksmiths' work, and what does the last line mean?

A shoemaker makes shoes without leather
With all the four elements put together:
Fire, Water, Earth, Air;
And every customer takes two pair.

3 The interesting sights and sounds of the smithy have found their way into several operas. One of the finest of these scenes is in *The Rhinegold*, by Richard Wagner. By adding to his large orchestra a collection of anvils — six small ones, six medium, and six large — Wagner has made a wonderful sound-picture of the underground smithies of the dwarfs ruled over by their harsh taskmaster Alberich. Another famous smithy scene is the anvil chorus in *Il trovatore*, by Giuseppe Verdi.

4 Practise *crescendos* and *decrescendos* with the hammering rhythms printed in this section.

5 This is the beginning of a long poem about the Cyclops, who were believed in ancient times to live near Mount Etna in Sicily. They were one-eyed giants, and in their smithies they made weapons for the gods, such as Jupiter's thunderbolts and Neptune's trident. The poem was written by Thomas Dekker, who lived in the days of Will Kemp.

Song of the Cyclops

Brave iron, brave hammer, from your sound
The art of music has her ground;
On the anvil thou keep'st time,
Thy knick-a-knock is a smith's best chime.
            Yet thwick-a-thwack, thwick, thwack-a-twack, thwack,
            Make our brawny sinews crack:
            Then pit-a-pat, pat, pit-a-pat, pat,
            Till thickest bars be beaten flat.

An English proverb: *Strike while the iron is hot!*
A French one: *C'est en forgeant qu'on devient forgeron.*

HOW SOUND TRAVELS

Vibrations make sound-waves in the air. Starting from whatever is vibrating — a tightly stretched violin string, or the air in a flute or trumpet, or the skin of a drum, or the metal of a triangle or bell — the sound-waves spread out and are caught by our ears. Sound waves do not travel as fast as light waves, which are so rapid that they reach our eyes almost instantly, unless they come from immense distances, like the light of the stars. Most of the sounds we hear, whether they are high or low, loud or soft, travel through the air at the rate of about 1,100 feet (or about 330 metres) a second. Sound travels more rapidly through water, and even faster through something solid like the ground, a wooden floor, an iron girder, or a steel wire.

The speed of sound several miles above the earth is slower, because the air is thinner and colder at those heights. At about six or seven miles up, sound travels at about 1,000 feet a second, or 660 miles an hour. This speed is now called Mach 1. Some jet aircraft fly at even greater speeds, which is why they are called supersonic (meaning 'beyond the speed of sound'). As the speed of such an aircraft increases past Mach 1, it pushes the sound waves before it and so builds up a 'sound barrier', which it breaks through with a noise that can be heard miles below on the earth; this is the 'sonic boom'.

Some problems to think about

1 Take a smooth wooden stick, about a metre in length, put one end of it close to your ear, and ask someone to scratch the stick near the other end. Then try the same experiment with a metal rod of about the same length. What difference do you notice in the sound, and how would you explain it?

2 Red Indians are said to have listened for the approach of enemies by putting their ears close to the ground. Why would this give a better warning than by listening in the ordinary way?

3 Why does the hum of an aircraft (at normal speeds, not supersonic ones) often seem to come from some distance behind it?

4 Why do we sometimes hear a clap of thunder several seconds after seeing a flash of lightning? Think of a way of reckoning how far away the storm is happening.

5 When a large number of people are singing together in a long church or hall, to the accompaniment of an organ or piano, those at the back find it hard to keep up with those near the front, where the instrument is. What is the reason for this 'dragging'?

SIGNALLING IN THE HILL COUNTRY

In the mountainous parts of Sweden and Norway, the cows, goats and sheep used to be taken early in the summer from the valley farms to fresh grazing land further up the hillside. The time to begin doing this was when the snow was disappearing from the slopes. But first of all bonfires were lit, to scare off imaginary creatures such as giants and trolls, or real enemies of the farm animals like wolves and bears. Before being driven into the hills, the cows had their horns decorated with garlands of wild flowers, a bell was fastened to the neck of the leading cow, and the young heifers that were going out for the first time were all given names.

The girls who looked after the herds knew they would be staying in the hills for most of the summer, and so they carried baskets on their backs, filled with spare clothing and food. But most of what they ate would be the milk and cheese provided by their animals. The herd-girls slept in huts made of logs with roofs of turf, earthern floors carpeted with branches of fir and pine that were changed every day, and a hearth of stones in the middle. The smoke from the wood fire had to find its way out through a hole left in the roof. Round the living-hut were other buildings to shelter the animals at night, and to store the milk and make cheese in.

As they might be living five miles or more from the nearest farm, the herd-girls were alone most of the time with the animals, though on Sundays their friends or families might climb the hills and visit them. To amuse themselves during the long summer days when they were out of doors with the herds, the girls liked to play on a pipe — a kind of recorder with six finger-holes but no thumb-hole. If they wanted to make louder music they used a hollow cow-horn or goat-horn with a few holes bored in it, or a home-made wooden trumpet called a *lur*. By playing on these instruments the herd-girls could signal to one another as each followed her animals from one patch of mountain grass to another. They used different tunes to convey messages, such as that an animal had strayed and must be looked out for, or that a missing animal had turned up, or that it was time for all to get together for the midday rest round a smoky wood fire lit to keep the midges off. The cows, goats and sheep were said to like the music of the little finger-pipe, while the harsher noises of the cow-horn or wooden *lur* had been known to scare off the dreaded wolf or bear.

Some of the signal-tunes had words, others none, but were understood all the same, like this minor tune which meant that a missing goat had been found:

Another tune, with words to sing to it, reported that a cow had strayed into a patch of woodland:

Lit - tle cow, lit - tle cow, lit - tle cow gone a - stray,

Lit - tle cow, lit - tle cow, lit - tle cow gone a - stray.

More than a hundred years ago, a Swedish clergyman living in the lovely mountain country of Dalarna described the end of a long summer day:

'When the sun begins to sink in the west, the herd-girls return with their animals. They come from all parts of the compass, happily singing . . .   The mountains echo with it, and deep in the forest it is heard by the toil-weary men folk.'

One of the home-going tunes he wrote down as he heard it had no words, but was either played or sung in a way that roused echoes among the rocks. Here it is arranged for a group of recorders, with a smaller group or a single recorder to imitate the answering echoes:

Among the strangest of the herd-girls' songs was the one called 'Twelve men'. There are various explanations of the words. One story tells how a herd-girl was attacked by cattle-robbers, but managed to signal with the *lur* to the men down in the valley, so that they came to her rescue. Another explanation is that the song gives warning that a bear has been sighted. The bear was so much feared that it was thought unlucky even to mention his name, so that he was referred to as *'Twelve men'* because of his strength.

Once again, the tune is a minor one, this time with E as *lah*.

At the end of the song you can see two chords, each with three notes in it; one is the *lah* chord, made up of E-G-B, and the other the *soh* chord, D-F sharp-A. If you can form teams of people to be ready with these two chords on chime bars or glockenspiels, you can try to fit one chord or the other to each bar of the tune. This will take a lot of preparation, but if you can get it right the sound will be quite magical.

TWELVE MEN

Lis - ten and hear me! Twelve men in the woods I see;

Twelve men all a - round, Sharp swords on them bound.

Great big ox - en they do drive; My bell - cow they'll take a - live.

My dog they will kill, And I fear they'll car - ry me a -

- way in - to the for - rest.

lah chord   *soh* chord

When the summer ended, the herd-girls left the mountain slopes and took the animals down to their winter quarters in stalls or byres. A Norwegian poet once imagined the mountain hut left empty and silent, with the turf withered brown on the roof, and no visitors except perhaps a mountain-spirit or *hulder.* The poem is fitted to a *lur*-call with only four different notes in it (notice how often the interval of a sixth makes a wonderfully haunting effect). At the end of the tune is printed a four-note chord (*doh-me-soh-lah,* G-B-D-E). If you can arrange for this to be played (or hummed) by a team, you will find that it fits the whole tune:

THE DESERTED MOUNTAIN HUT

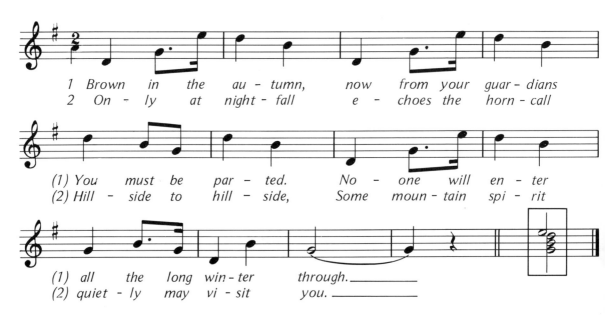

1 Brown in the au - tumn, now from your guar - dians
2 On - ly at night - fall e - choes the horn - call

(1) You must be par - ted. No - one will en - ter
(2) Hill - side to hill - side, Some moun - tain spi - rit

(1) all the long win - ter through.
(2) quiet - ly may vi - sit you.

Reproduced by permission of the Swiss National Tourist Office

Norway and Sweden were not the only countries where mountain dwellers signalled to one another by means of instruments and voices. The Swiss or Austrian *alphorn* is much larger than the *lur;* some alphorns are ten feet long and make a tremendous sound among the mountains. The Swiss and Austrian mountain people also learnt to sing in a special way called *yodelling.* This popular song from Switzerland has a yodelling chorus:

FROM LUCERNE
TO WEGGIS' STRAND

Things to do

1 Find out more about summer pasture life in the Scandinavian countries, Sweden and Norway. The summer huts were called *säters* or *seters*. There are not many of the old ones left, now that more modern methods of sheep-rearing and dairy-farming are used. But some of the *seters* have been turned into holiday cabins, or new wooden huts can be rented in the *seter* districts. There are more herd-girls' songs and pipe-tunes in a booklet called *Old Mountain Tunes from Sweden*.

2 The music of the mountain-peoples has found its way into some exciting pieces for orchestra; one of the most famous is the Overture to *William Tell*, an opera by Rossini, which uses some of the cow-calling tunes known in Switzerland as *Ranz des vaches*.

3 We have mentioned the sixths in the melody of 'The deserted mountain hut'. The yodels in 'From Lucerne to Weggis' Strand' have not only sixths, but also sevenths, which are quite hard to sing until you get the knack of them. Men use a special kind of voice, called *falsetto*, when yodelling the wider intervals.

USING THE BASS CLEF

Let us first of all check the letter names of all the notes we have been reading and writing on the stave, without troubling about sharps or flats for the time being. We start from the G line, because it is clearly signalled by the G clef, and go steadily upwards, using every line and every space. In this way we can get in a whole octave of notes, plus an extra A with a leger line to itself:

Now we start from 'clef' G again, and track the scale downwards. This time there are fewer lines and spaces, and to finish on C we have to put in another leger line:

Find that leger-line C on the piano keyboard. It is the one nearest to the lock of the piano lid, and is often called 'middle C'. When you have found it, look at all the black and white keys stretching leftwards, down below middle C. If we want to write any of those lower sounds we shall have to put in some more leger lines:

But even now we have not gone nearly far enough to write still deeper sounds, such as those sung by men's voices or played on instruments like the cello or by the pianist's left hand. Yet too many leger lines are a nuisance to keep writing, and they make the notes hard to read.

There is, however, a way to solve this problem. What we do is to take another clef, called the bass or F clef, and fix it round the *fourth* line of the stave:

This F shows exactly the same sound as the three-leger-line F we have just seen written, but it is much more convenient. It needs no leger lines, and there is still plenty of room on the stave to go down a whole octave:

There is room at the top also for four useful notes:

The bass clef began its life as a capital F, but through being written by hand so many times its shape got changed. The upright stroke of the F grew crooked and the side-strokes turned into dots.

Remember that these dots must go one on each side of the fourth line.

For some practice in working with the bass clef, here is a Yugoslav song. It is full of a catchy rhythm that is not at all hard to get hold of if you remember the Morse Code signal for letter R, which is • —— • (dot-dash-dot, short-long-short, or in musical notes quaver-crotchet-quaver:

THE HUSSARS ARE COMING

1 Hey! Do you hear them, the hooves of their hor-ses, the
2 Hey! Do you see them, the gal-lop-ing sol-diers, the a –
3 Give them a cheer then, and show them they're wel-come, and

(1) jin-gle of har-ness, the rat-tle of sa-bres? The
(2) -stride of their hor-ses, their hel-mets all flash-ing? The
(3) strike up the mu-sic, and join them in danc-ing. The

(1) hus-sars are com-ing this way to our vil-lage.
(2) hus-sars are com-ing this way to our vil-lage.
(3) hus-sars are stay-ing this night in our vil-lage.

40

Things to do

1 When you know the tune and words of 'The hussars are coming', try adding percussion parts to it. Jingling instruments like tambourines and triangles will sound right, with wood-blocks or coconut shells to imitate horse-hooves. These time-patterns would all fit:

quaver-quaver-crotchet

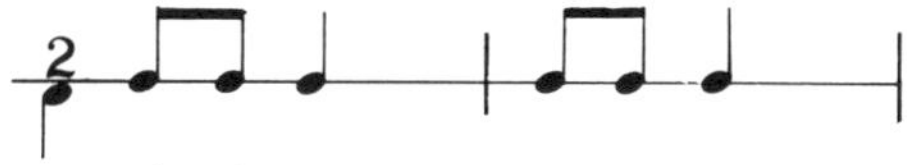

quaver-crotchet-quaver

crotchet on the second beat only

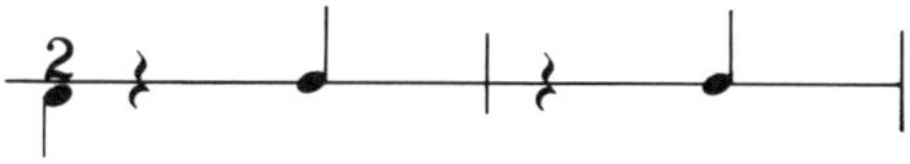

2 Practise making the bass clef. Its crooked back looks like a C turned the wrong way. Then come the two dots: 𝄢

3 Work out the letter names of these three notes (the third is the lowest note of the cello):

4 Do these two notes show different sounds, or the same one?

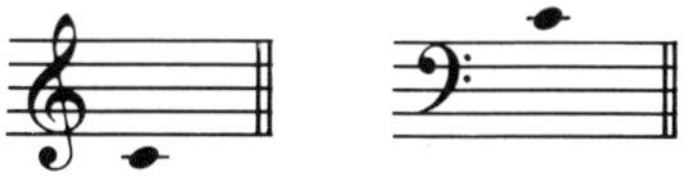

5 *A problem for those interested in mathematics* **If** this sound is made by a string vibrating 350 times a second

 how many vibrations will make this sound:

 and this one:  ?

6 The key signatures hoisted at the beginning of a tune in the bass clef will have their sharps and flats in positions different from those we are used to with the treble clef. Look at these, and work out why the change of clef makes them all different:

CANALS

Man-made waterways, called canals, were first dug for drainage and transport in level districts, and for irrigation or supplying crops with water. Later on, the drilling of tunnels and the invention of locks and boat-lifts made it possible to construct them even in hilly regions.

Some of the oldest and most famous canals in Europe are those of Venice, where they took the place of main streets and came to be lined with splendid palaces and churches. Beautifully-shaped and decorated boats, known as gondolas, carried passengers up and down and across the waterways from one part of Venice to another. There are still some rowed gondolas, though most of the water traffic is now carried on by motor launches. Part of the attractiveness of the old gondolas was that the boatmen, or 'gondoliers', sang at their work, sometimes even sharing a song with a partner in another boat, and it was worth travelling by gondola to hear them. As an Italian word for boat is *barca*, a boatman's song was often called a *barcarolle.* Here is one that used to be sung by two gondoliers, though the words show that it is really a conversation between a fisherman and a girl who has lost her ring in the canal. We have printed the tune with both treble and bass clefs, so that you can sing it as a duet if you like:

O FISHERMAN, COME IN FROM SEA

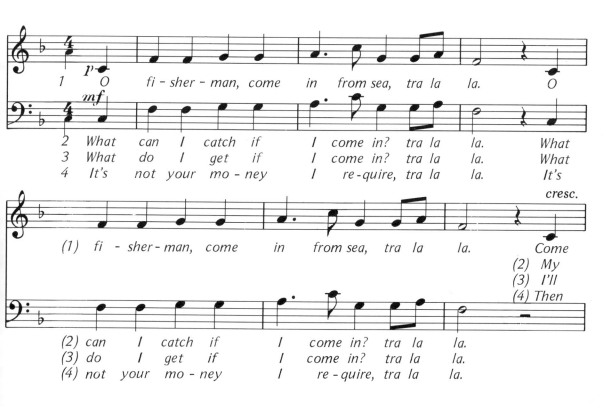

1. O fi-sher-man, come in from sea, tra la la. O
2. What can I catch if I come in? tra la la. What
3. What do I get if I come in? tra la la. What
4. It's not your mo-ney I re-quire, tra la la. It's

cresc.

(1) fi-sher-man, come in from sea, tra la la. Come
(2) My
(3) I'll
(4) Then

(2) can I catch if I come in? tra la la.
(3) do I get if I come in? tra la la.
(4) not your mo-ney I re-quire, tra la la.

(1) row your boat through the wa - ter, and come and fish with
(2) gol - den ring in the wa - ter, so come and fish with
(3) give you plen - ty of mo - ney, so come and fish with
(4) take my thanks for your kind - ness, and come and fish with

(1) me, I say, and come and fish with me,
(2) me, I say, so come and fish with me,
(3) me, I say, so come and fish with me,
(4) me, I say, and come and fish with me,
tra la la la la la la.

(end of verse 4)   tra la la la la la la.

In the eastern parts of Britain canals were introduced four hundred years ago, chiefly to drain marshy land and prevent flooding. Some of the men who planned and carried out the work were brought over from Holland, a country that had long experience in making artificial waterways, and where much traffic still goes by water. But the great age of canal-building or 'navigation' began in our country after the year 1760, and owed much to a skilful water-engineer named James Brindley. By joining river to river all over the land, Brindley and other engineers provided a network of 'liquid roads', along which horse-drawn barges carried coal, iron, clay, bricks, slates, timber, grain and other raw materials, with manufactured goods and food for the growing towns. A canal finished in 1772 to join Wolverhampton and Birmingham had a song of its own made about it:

THE NEW NAVIGATION

1 This day for our new na-vi - ga-tion___ We ba-nish all care and vex -
2 Not Europe can match us for traffic,___ A - me - ri - ca, A - sia, or

(1) - a-tion;___ The sight of the bar-ges each ho-nest heart glows, And the
(2) A-fric;___ Of what we in-vent each par - takes of a share, For the

(1) mer-riest of mor-tals are Bir-ming-ham lads, Bir-ming-ham lads,
(2) best of wrought metals is Bir-ming-ham ware, Bir-ming-ham ware,

(1) jo - vi - al blades, And the mer-riest of mor-tals are Bir-ming-ham lads.
(2) none is so rare, For the best of wrought metals is Bir-ming-ham ware.

Since then, broader and deeper canals have been cut to join rivers, lakes, and even oceans. One of the longest of the early American man-made waterways was the Erie Canal, completed in 1825. It joined Lake Erie with the Hudson river and stretched for nearly four hundred miles, with 83 locks to climb the hills and 18 aqueducts to carry the canal across rivers. The whole journey from Albany, on the Hudson River north of New York, to Buffalo on Lake Erie took about nine days. Whole families lived on the boats and helped to work them, with horses or mules to supply the power. There is a fine song about the Erie Canal, one version of which goes like this:

THE ERIE CANAL

I've got a mule, her name is Sal: Fif-teen miles on the E-rie Ca-nal. She's a good old wor-ker, a good old pal: Fif-teen miles on the E-rie Ca-nal. We've hauled some bar-ges in our day, Filled with lum-ber, coal and hay, And we know ev'-ry

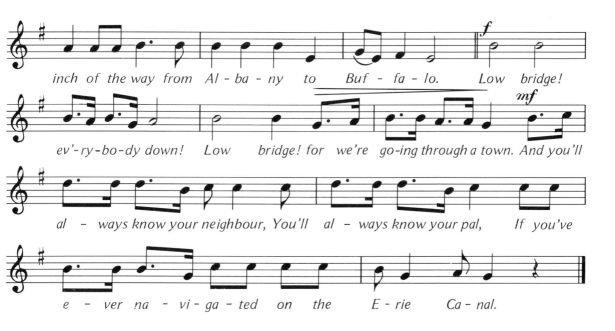

inch of the way from Al - ba - ny   to   Buf - fa - lo.   Low   bridge!

ev'-ry-bo-dy down!   Low   bridge! for we're go-ing through a town. And you'll

al - ways know your neighbour, You'll   al - ways know your pal,   If you've

e - ver na - vi - ga - ted   on   the   E - rie   Ca - nal.

Another popular old American song may be about river boatmen and not canal crews, but it is so lively and tuneful that it seems worth putting in here:

THE BOATMAN'S DANCE

1   The boat-man_dance, the_ boat-man_ sing, The boat-man up to_
2   The boat-man_came with a new frock coat, The boat-man came with a
3   O-ver the moun-tains, slick as an eel, The boat-man slide down

(1) ev' - ry - thing. And when the boat - man gets on shore, He'll
(2) five pound note; Stand back, young man, you've got no chance, For
(3) on his heel. The schoo-ner sails be - fore the wind, The

(1) spend his mo-ney then work for more.
(2) this don't make_ the boat-man dance. } O dance, boat-man dance,
(3) steamboat leaves_ a trail be-hind.

dance, boat - man dance, dance all night till the

broad day-light And go home with the girls in the morn - ing.

Things to do

1 There is almost sure to be a canal not too far from where you live. Find out all you can about it: when it was made, what towns or rivers it connects, what kind of goods it carried, and whether it is still in use, either for industry or for people to spend holidays on. Find out also how a lock works, and what an aqueduct is like.

2 In the busiest canal-making days, a man who worked with pick and shovel at digging canals, or laying roads and (later on) railways, was often called a 'navvy'. Can you explain how this word came to be used? In time 'steam navvies' were invented. What kind of machine is now used instead?

3 Find out more about the canals of (a) Holland, (b) Venice, and (c) East Anglia and the Fen Country.

4 Use maps to trace the course of the Erie Canal. There is a fine picture book about it, illustrated by Peter Spier. It brings everything to life in coloured drawings — the boats, the horses and mules, the boatmen and their families, the goods carried, and the shops and other buildings that grew up on the shores of the canal. Try to get this book through your school or public library. (The version of the song given at the back of the book is not quite the same as ours.)

5 Learn something of the history of the huge canals joining the oceans — the Suez and the Panama Canals. The latter is one of the largest man-made waterways in the world, but work on it nearly came to a standstill through the activities of one of the smallest creatures, the mosquito.

6 Many pieces of music have the title *Barcarolle*. A pianist who has reached Grade 5 or beyond could manage some of those composed by Tchaikovsky and Mendelssohn. Other more difficult ones are on records.

Salisbury Cathedral with rainbow, painted by JOHN CONSTABLE (1776-1837)

THE SOUND RAINBOW

The great mathematician and scientist, Sir Isaac Newton, showed that what we call 'white' light is really made up of colours — red, orange, yellow, green, blue, indigo, and violet. He proved this by allowing a beam of sunlight to pass through a piece of triangular glass, or prism, and observing the whole range of colours thrown upon a screen. We now know that each colour has its own wavelength — for light, like sound, is produced by wave-movement, and that there are wavelengths that our eyes cannot detect, called the infra-red and ultra-violet rays. Anyone can repeat Newton's experiment with the prism, or we can reverse it by spinning a disc or top marked with the separate colours or 'spectrum', and seeing how they mix together as a white surface. The most beautiful spectrum of all is the rainbow, seen after a shower of rain; the millions of drops of water in the air act as a mass of tiny prisms, breaking up the light of the sun into a great arch of colours.

What seems to be a single clear musical note is nearly always a cloud or mixture of many different sounds. A voice or instrument produces a main sound which we can hear plainly, but along with it there are many higher sounds, all very faint and some we cannot hear at all, though scientists can prove they are there. We call this cloud of sounds the *harmonics* of the main note. Not only do they make the main sound richer and brighter, but they also enable us to tell a violin from a flute, or a piano from a trumpet, even though they are all playing the same note. The reason for these differences of 'tone-colour' between one instrument and another is that each kind of instrument gives certain harmonics that are a little stronger than the rest. The louder and lower the main sound is, the easier it is to hear the harmonics.

Some experiments with harmonics

Experiment 1 Open the top of a piano, and stand close to it so that you can hear what happens inside. Get someone to press down the *right* (or 'damper') pedal, so that all the strings of the piano are free to vibrate. Now find the lowest C on the keyboard, strike it firmly, and listen hard. You will hear, humming quietly above the loud C you have struck:

many other C's higher up the piano
some of the G's

and (if you have keen ears) perhaps some E's and a few other fainter harmonics. This cloud of sounds, floating along with the main deep note, is called *the harmonic series*.

Experiment 2 Your partner should now release the pedal so that the pads or 'dampers' drop on to the strings and stop their vibrations. Then, after putting the pedal down afresh, repeat Experiment 1 with another deep note — say D this time. You will then hear a different harmonic series:

some more D's
some A's
and perhaps some F sharps

Experiment 3 For the next set of experiments you will need a violin or cello and the help of someone who knows a little about playing a stringed instrument. Remember that when a stretched string vibrates it moves very rapidly from side to side. It is quite possible sometimes to see this happening. But what we cannot see, and what is hard to understand or even believe, is that the string is not only vibrating through its whole length, but at the same time in two halves, in three thirds, in four quarters, and so on in smaller and smaller fractions. Each fraction makes its own sound, though very faintly. These vibrations of fractions of the string make up its harmonic series, or 'sound rainbow'. Now this is where your expert comes in. He will know the trick of making the harmonics sound separately, like each of the colours of the rainbow. He does this by touching the string at exactly half way along, or a third, or a quarter or other fraction. The string then stops vibrating along its full length and only the harmonic is heard, as a clear sweet note.

For example, if the D string is touched in the middle and made to vibrate with the bow, it will sound the D an octave higher. Touched so that it vibrates in quarters, it will give the D an octave higher still. If touched to make it vibrate in thirds, it will sound the harmonic A midway between the two high D's:

D ½ ⅓ ¼
(MAIN NOTE)

The harmonics of brass wind instruments

When the air inside a tube vibrates, it does so along the whole length of the tube, but at the same time in fractions also, like a stretched string. This is harder to imagine even than with the string, but it is quite true. A trumpet player is able to tighten or slacken his lips on the mouthpiece, and in that way pick out several of the harmonics separately. For example, if the main note of his trumpet is C, he can sound these five harmonics:

As you can see at once, this is not a scale, because there are gaps in the ladder between one harmonic and the next. For centuries brass instruments like trumpets and horns had to make do with the few notes that could be produced with the lips, though some players became extremely clever at picking out higher and higher harmonics; it is a fact that the higher you go in the harmonic series the closer the notes come together, so that the best players could manage nearly all the notes of the scale if they went high enough. Nowadays brass players fill in the gaps with less effort by incorporating additional tubing by the operation of valves fitted to their instruments. But the bugle is still without valves, which is why bugle calls are always made out of the same few notes, all of them harmonics. This call was used for many years in the British army as a fire alarm; the words underneath were sometimes given as a help in teaching young buglers:

FIRE ALARM

(Fire, fire, fire! Fire, fire, fire! Fire, fire, fire! Come on o-ver, come on o-ver, come and put it out!)

The harmonics of recorders

We have to use harmonics to make many of the higher sounds on the recorder. This means doing several things at once — partly uncovering the thumb-hole, using extra breath-pressure, and learning new fingerings, so that it needs much time and patience to be sure of these higher notes. A book on recorder playing, like *The Recorder in School* by Freda Dinn, will give a great deal of help.

A strange instrument

There is one curious little instrument that depends on harmonics for *all* its notes. This is the so-called 'jew's harp'; how it got that name is not clear, for there is nothing Jewish about it and it is not a harp. Some people think the name is a mistake for 'jaw's harp'. It is a thin tongue of steel fixed to a small frame. You play it by holding the frame and twanging the metal tongue near your half-open teeth, so that it vibrates and makes a twanging or buzzing sound. This sound has its own 'rainbow' of harmonics, which would be very faint indeed from so small an instrument, but your mouth acts like a cavern and magnifies the harmonics. By altering the shape of your lips, tongue and teeth (as if you are saying different words) you can pick out first one harmonic and then another, until with practice you can produce something like a tune. This is a very ancient instrument, found in many parts of the world under different names. In Scotland it used to be played for dancing, and in Austria for young men to serenade their girl friends. You can buy a 'jew's harp' in most music shops.

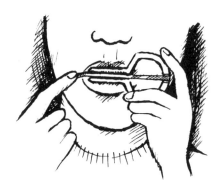

A sound rainbow

Here is part of a sound rainbow — the first twelve notes of the harmonic series of C on the second leger line below the stave with the bass clef. This happens to be the lowest note of the cello. Find it on the piano keyboard. Notice how many C's these twelve notes include. The B flat and the F sharp are slightly different from those notes in our modern system of tuning:

TOWNS BENEATH THE SEA

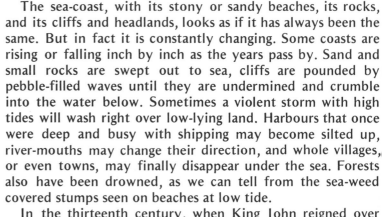

The sea-coast, with its stony or sandy beaches, its rocks, and its cliffs and headlands, looks as if it has always been the same. But in fact it is constantly changing. Some coasts are rising or falling inch by inch as the years pass by. Sand and small rocks are swept out to sea, cliffs are pounded by pebble-filled waves until they are undermined and crumble into the water below. Sometimes a violent storm with high tides will wash right over low-lying land. Harbours that once were deep and busy with shipping may become silted up, river-mouths may change their direction, and whole villages, or even towns, may finally disappear under the sea. Forests also have been drowned, as we can tell from the sea-weed covered stumps seen on beaches at low tide.

In the thirteenth century, when King John reigned over England, the city of Dunwich on the coast of Suffolk was a busy and prosperous place with a harbour and docks that could shelter seventy vessels, with town walls and gates, a market place, nine churches, and its own mint for making coinage. Today all that is left to remind us of Dunwich are a few gravestones on a cliff top. Storm after storm carried away land and buildings. In 1344 the sea swallowed up four hundred houses. One night in 1677 the inhabitants awoke to find salt waves washing through the market place. In the course of the next hundred years the rest of the town had vanished — walls, churches, and the last remaining houses.

There are stories of other sunken regions in Britain, such as Cardigan Bay, where according to legend as many as sixteen cities lie beneath the sea not far from the modern town of Aberdovey; Kenfig in South Wales; and the ancient vanished land of Lyonesse off the rocky coast of Cornwall. Across the English Channel, off the coast of Brittany, is the drowned kingdom of Ys, which was said to rise to the surface of the water every Easter Day, with the bells of all its churches ringing joyfully.

Things to do

1 Find out if there are any tales of drowned land in your own district. In modern times an inland valley may have been flooded intentionally, by building a dam across it in order to form a reservoir.

2 Find out something about the strangest of all legends of drowned land, the tale of the continent of Atlantis, which was said to have sunk in very ancient times below the waters of the ocean that now bears its name, the Atlantic.

3 Ring a bell (an old school 'yard bell' would be about the right size), and while it is still vibrating lower it into a bowl of water. Listen to what happens to the sound.

4 Make a sound-picture of the bells of a sunken city, tolling under the waves, and then rising out of them like the bells of Ys on Easter Day. Use chime bars or tubular bells, and try striking them in pairs with two beaters. Notes a fifth apart can suggest tolling bells, because the interval of a fifth is one of the easiest sounds to hear as harmonics:

You might also use the French bell-chime printed on page 9 of Book 1, adding fifths and octaves above it if you like:

To represent the sea washing over the hidden city, try sliding wooden beaters gently up and down all the notes of a xylophone or glockenspiel. This effect is called *glissando*, and is sometimes shown in writing by means of a wavy line:

Think of other sounds you could add to the picture, for example stones, pebbles, and sand shaken together.

Finally, the whole piece can be recorded on tape.

5 Those who enjoy painting could choose as a subject the buildings of a town lying beneath the sea.

6 Read the North Country legend, *The Ballad of Semmerwater*, as told in verse by William Watson, and afterwards turn the story into a series of paintings or into a sound-picture with speech and music, like a radio script. (There are a few North Country words that may need explanation: *mickle* means 'great', *brant* means 'steep')

60

The Ballad of Semmerwater

Deep asleep, deep asleep,
Deep asleep it lies,
The still lake of Semmerwater
Under the still skies.

And many a fathom, many a fathom,
Many a fathom below,
In a king's tower and a queen's bower
The fishes come and go.

Once there stood by Semmerwater
A mickle town and tall;
King's tower and queen's bower,
And wakeman on the wall.

Came a beggar halt and sore:
'I faint for lack of bread.'
King's tower and queen's bower
Cast him forth unfed.

He knocked at the door of the herdman's cot
The herdman's cot in the dale.
They gave him of their oatcake,
They gave him of their ale.

He has cursed aloud that city proud,
He has cursed it in its pride;
He has cursed it into Semmerwater
Down the brant hillside;
He has cursed it into Semmerwater
There to bide.

King's tower and queen's bower,
And a mickle town and tall;
By glimmer of scale and gleam of fin,
Folk have seen them all.
King's tower and queen's bower,
And weed and reed in the gloom.
And a lost city in Semmerwater,
Deep asleep till Doom.

As a change from making ladders or scales that move up and down in a mixture of large and small steps (tones and semitones), it is interesting to build a scale out of nothing but semitones. Use the piano keyboard, or a glockenspiel or xylophone if you have a chromatic one (with a double row of notes), or a complete chromatic set of chime bars. Start from 'middle C' and move upwards (to the right), touching every white and black key or bar, taking them in order and not missing out any, until you arrive at a C again. Then do the same thing backwards — from the upper C to the lower one, again touching every key or bar on the way.

Count how many keys you touch in going up or coming down. Not counting the C you finish on, you will find you have touched twelve. We call this a chromatic scale.

There are various ways of writing a chromatic scale on the stave, but the simplest one is to write notes with sharps before them when going up, and notes with flats when coming down:

Notice these points:

1 The notes with sharps or flats before them are the sounds produced by the black keys. (This is true if we start and finish on C, but the rule has to be changed a little if we choose some other note to begin with.)

2 There are no black keys on the piano between E and F, and B and C. Why not?

3 Every black key can have two names — a sharp name and a flat name.
Find the flat names for: C sharp
                             D sharp
                             F sharp
                             G sharp
                             A sharp

Theseus, Ariadne and the Labyrinth

63

THE MAZE AND THE MINOTAUR

Thousands of years ago a rich and powerful king is said to have ruled over the large island of Crete in the Mediterranean Sea. His name was Minos. His ships traded and made war far and wide over the Mediterranean, and peoples in distant lands were forced to pay him tribute.

At Knossos in Crete we can see the ruins of a vast royal palace which may have been the centre of Minos' empire. According to legend, some of the buildings were designed by a craftsman called Daedalus. He was believed to have invented, among other things, the potter's wheel, the first pair of compasses for marking out circles, and the first saw for cutting wood, which he made by copying in iron the backbone of a large fish. Minos ordered Daedalus to construct a maze of rooms and passages, called a labyrinth, leading to a den in the middle where the king kept a savage monster, half man and half bull, known as the Minotaur.

Every ninth year the people of Athens, far away on the mainland of Greece, had to send as tribute to Minos seven of their young men and seven young women. When these arrived in Crete they would be thrust into the labyrinth, to wander hopelessly in and out of its dark passages until they were at last caught and devoured by the Minotaur.

But one year, when the time for sending the tribute came round again, a brave man named Theseus volunteered to take the place of one of the lads doomed to be sacrificed. He took two other strong young men with him to help, disguising them as two of the girls. Then they all set off from Athens in a ship rowed by thirty oarsmen and fitted with masts and sails. The sails were black, according to the usual custom at this sad time, but Theseus promised that if he were successful in destroying the Minotaur and bringing back his companions they would change the sails on the homeward voyage for white ones.

Soon after landing in Crete they were all taken before Minos to be counted and sent to their fate. Standing near the king's throne was the royal princess, Ariadne. She at once fell in love with Theseus, and made up her mind to help the captives to escape. She knew the dangers of the labyrinth, and how no one had ever found the way out again. In secret she gave Theseus a sword and a ball of woollen thread from her spinning-room. Following her directions, Theseus fastened one end of the thread to a hook near the entrance to the labyrinth, and as he and his companions crept further and further into the maze he unrolled the ball, so that however much the passages twisted and turned he would always have a clue to finding his way back to the entrance. When at last they could hear the growls of the Minotaur, Theseus and his two chosen helpers went on ahead, found the monster, and slew it with the sword. Then they went back to where the rest of the victims waited, and Theseus led them all safely out of the labyrinth by winding up Ariadne's thread.

Helped again by Ariadne, the young people of Athens escaped from the palace and found their way down to the sea, where their ship had been secretly waiting in the faint hope that some at least of the captives might return. Before embarking they all took part in a joyful dance, imitating the windings of the labyrinth and led by Ariadne, who had begged to leave Crete and sail home with them. But in their excitement they forgot to change the sails for white ones, and the king of Athens, seeing the vessel approaching with its black sails still spread, died of grief.

For long afterwards, however, the story of Theseus' courage and Ariadne's clever device of the thread were remembered every year in the winding dance.

Things to do

1 Look at the picture on page 63. This is what an Italian artist five hundred years ago imagined the labyrinth would have been like. He made it like a castle of his own time, and dressed Theseus and Ariadne in the costumes of great people whom he knew. See if you can trace the way to the centre of the labyrinth, and then out again. Ariadne (on the right) is handing Theseus a ball of wool, and another part of the picture shows that he has tied the end of the thread to a ring by the gateway and is going inside. The ship with black sails is also shown. On the left we see a part of the story that comes later; Ariadne, left alone on a desert island, is signalling for help, and the god Zeus (with wings) rescues her from the sea and carries her up into the sky, to shine for ever as a starry crown. In the top right hand corner, Daedalus and his son Icarus are trying to escape from Minos by means of wings that Daedalus has made for them, but Icarus' wings have given way and he has fallen into the waves, with only his legs showing.

2 There are other stories connected with Theseus, Ariadne, and Daedalus. One tells how Daedalus was given the task of threading a spiral shell (like a whelk shell). This is nearly impossible, as you will soon realise if you try it, but Daedalus performed it successfully by fastening the thread to a small beetle and sending her into the winding passages of the shell.

3 Labyrinths and mazes are a wonderfully interesting subject. There are outdoor mazes, like the one in the grounds of Hampton Court Palace, and indoor ones, like the mirror halls in fairs and amusement shows; maze designs, maze puzzles in books and magazines, puzzle toys where you have to get a ball through a maze, and mazes you can invent for yourselves with pencil and paper. There are even mazes in some churches, like the one you can walk round just inside the west door of Ely Cathedral.

4 Begin to build up a sound picture following the story of Theseus, Ariadne, and the Minotaur. Here are some ideas to work on: *The sea,* with the waves, the ship, and the swish of thirty pairs of oars. Invent a rowing tune in $\frac{6}{8}$ time, like this one from the Aran islands off the west coast of Ireland. (This melody, or your own, could be given a live or taped background of moving water):

King Minos As a royal person, his presence could be shown by trumpet calls and solemn percussion rhythms.

The Minotaur Roaring or growling sounds could be made with large drums, or voices amplified through cardboard tubes. There is actually a very old instrument, called the bull-roarer, which is found in several parts of the world among races such as the native peoples of Australia, the Navajo Indians of North America, and some Central African tribes. There are directions for making a bull-roarer in *The Oxford Companion to Music* (under the heading *Thunder Stick, Bull Roarer or Whizzer*). It is not hard to make, but be very careful how you use it, or someone might get hurt by the whirling board.

A sad song, for the voyage from Athens to Crete. It could be sung by boys and girls, like a two-part round, to the sound *ah*:

lah te doh ray me fah   me ray doh   te lah   (etc.)

lah   te doh   ray me fah   me ray doh   te   lah

A cheerful song, for the journey back to Athens. This could be the same round as before, but altered from the mournful minor to the brighter major:

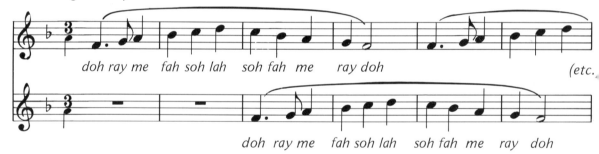

doh ray me   fah soh lah   soh fah me   ray doh   (etc.)

doh ray me   fah soh lah   soh fah me   ray doh

The Labyrinth A musical maze can be made out of the twelve semitones of the chromatic scale, arranged in a planned order. The easiest way to do this is with chime bars, if you are lucky enough to have a complete chromatic set. In that case you can experiment with putting them in different orders until you have made a series of sounds you like (musicans call this a note-series or tone-row). There are literally thousands of possibilities, as twelve different notes can be arranged in $1 \times 2 \times 3 \times 4 \times 5 \times 6 \times 7 \times 8 \times 9 \times 10 \times 11 \times 12$ ways, which is not a sum easily worked out in one's head! Here is just one of these arrangements; notice that we can use either sharps or flats in making a chromatic maze or note series, or a mixture of sharps and flats:

Forwards → ← Backwards

1 2 3 4 5 6 7 8 9 10 11 12

Ariadne's thread This will of course follow your 12-note series as the captives go into the maze. Coming out again, after the destruction of the Minotaur, the thread will be followed backwards, and the series played in reverse.

The dance The dance kept up by generations of Greek youths and girls in memory of Theseus' exploit was sometimes called the Crane Dance. We have no music for this, but there is a very popular dance-song from Crete, called *Pentozali,* which you can sing or play (or both). Add percussion instruments to mark the rhythm: suitable ones might be tambourine, small drums, triangles, ordinary cymbals, and the small cymbals sometimes called antique cymbals or 'Indian bells'.

PENTOZALI

1 Like cher-ries in the month of May, With sun-light on them
2 You men of Crete who watch the dance, Re - mem-ber how to
3 And while the Cre-tan mai-dens sing, Re - solve that ev' - ry

(1) glan - cing, You see how, join-ing hand in hand, The girls of Crete are
(2) che - rish The cus-toms of your an - ces-tors, And ne - ver let them
(3) na - tion Shall learn the mean-ing of the dance, And all its re - pu -

69

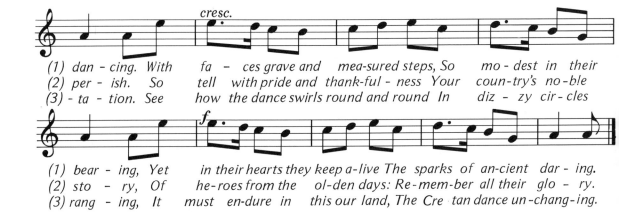

(1) dan - cing. With fa – ces grave and mea-sured steps, So mo - dest in their
(2) per - ish. So tell with pride and thank-ful - ness Your coun-try's no -ble
(3) - ta - tion. See how the dance swirls round and round In diz - zy cir - cles

(1) bear - ing, Yet in their hearts they keep a-live The sparks of an-cient dar - ing.
(2) sto - ry, Of he-roes from the ol-den days: Re-mem-ber all their glo - ry.
(3) rang - ing, It must en-dure in this our land, The Cre tan dance un-chang-ing.

RICHARD THE LION-HEART

Three English kings have been named Richard. The first of them, who reigned for ten years from 1189 to 1199, was sometimes called Richard Coeur-de-Lion or Richard the Lion-Heart. He had been brought up in France, and spoke French more naturally than English. He earned his nickname of 'Lion-Heart' through his courage in warfare, both in France in his younger days, and later in the Crusades. The Crusades were wars against the Turkish armies which had captured Jerusalem, with its holy places that were sacred to the Christian world.

Richard was crowned King of England at Westminster Abbey on Sunday 3 September, 1189. It was a gorgeous ceremony, as we can see from a brightly painted picture in a hand-written book made soon afterwards. We also have a song that was probably sung in the procession as it left the Abbey after the coronation and moved slowly back to the Palace of Westminster for a feast:

EARTH'S REBORN

Earth's re - born, the gold - en age Comes a - gain, peace bring - ing. Now are rich men trod - den down, Poor men raised with sing - ing. All the peo - ple greet their Prince, With his prai - ses ring - ing.

Nor is there a place for crime; Crime is____ ba-nished

for all____ time, E - vil thoughts sent____ wing - ing.

At the end of the song all the instruments,
which included pipes, harps and bells, struck
up a lively march:

RICHARD'S CORONATION MARCH

73

The King must have enjoyed his coronation music, because he was himself a poet and singer, or *trouvère* as it was called in French, and he always had his minstrels about him when he made journeys for peace or war into distant lands.

Soon after the coronation was over, Richard set out to join other kings and their armies on a Crusade that was to last three years. In warfare the Christian armies used trumpets and horns to signal to one another and to arouse their courage, but the Turkish armies had other instruments, many of them strange to western eyes and ears. Some of the Turkish instruments, such as *shawms*, or screaming reed-pipes, booming kettle-drums, and tinkling bell-chimes and cymbals, as well as the quieter instruments of their palaces and houses, like the lute, were captured and taken home by the Crusaders, and became popular in western countries. Here is an old tune said to be Turkish. You might try playing it on recorders, with percussion like cymbals, drums, and triangles to imitate the strange sounds Richard's men heard when the Turkish soldiers went into battle:

TURKISH MARCH

Everyone agreed that Richard was a brave fighter, but he was also proud and quarrelsome, and often fell out with other leaders on his own side. So it happened that on the long journey home across Europe, when the wars were ended, Richard was captured by a powerful lord and imprisoned in a strong castle in Austria. His captor demanded a large sum of money for his ransom — a hundred thousand pounds — and until it could be collected Richard had to spend many weary months in his prison cell. He sent messengers to France and England for the money, but he had already taxed his people heavily to pay for the Crusade, and they were slow in answering his appeal. In the meantime, Richard composed a song about the sad fate of a royal prisoner:

HOW CAN I TELL
OF A PRISONER'S FATE?

How can I tell of a pri - son - er's fate?

I must in song all my suff'- rings re - late.

Sad is my heart, for my ran - som I sigh. Ma - ny my

friends, but the price is too high. Will they not help me my

free - dom __ to gain? Or must I __ ask in vain?

There is a legend that one of Richard's friends, another
trouvère named Blondel, wandered from country to country

and castle to castle, trying to discover where the King was held captive. Wherever he went he kept singing the first line or two of one of Richard's own songs, and then listened carefully. He went on doing this until one day from the narrow window of a castle tower came the faint voice of the King himself, joining in with the rest of the verse. It is a good story, but unlikely to be true, though Blondel was a real person, and Richard in the end did gain his freedom and made his way back to England.

But he was soon at war again, this time not with the Turks but with other enemies he had made nearer home, in France. And in that country he met his death from a crossbow fired by a French soldier. It is said that when the man was seized and brought before the dying King, Richard pardoned him and ordered him to be set free. Another noble poet and musician, Gaucelm Faidit, composed a song mourning the death of Richard Coeur-de-Lion, and calling him 'the fountain-head and measure of all valour'.

Things to do

1 Find out more about the Crusades, and the people who took part in them on both sides, including Richard's chief opponent, Saladin. There are many interesting things to learn about the changes the Crusades brought about in western lands, affecting not only methods of warfare but also styles of building, furniture, food, fashions in dress, musical instruments, and games: chess, for example, was brought from the east, and in that game we still use the words *check mate* which come from eastern languages and mean 'the king is dead'.

2 Royal or knightly poets and musicians were called troubadours in the southern part of France, trouvères in the north. Richard and Blondel were trouvères. Both troubadours and trouvères may sometimes have composed the melodies of their songs, but it is more probable that they made up new words to old tunes which they learned from their minstrels. Here is a very beautiful trouvère melody that can be played on a descant recorder with left-hand fingers only. The minstrels usually played on the harp to accompany their singing, and you could imitate this by twanging two notes (*doh* and

soh) on the two middle strings of a cello:

or the lowest strings of a violin:

or by striking two chime bars or glockenspiel notes:

TROUVÈRE MELODY ('God of love')

3 Look at the picture on page 74. The upper part of it shows Crusaders fighting with Turkish warriors (how can you tell which are which?), while below two men are relaxing in their tent over a game of chess.